Crocodiles

Victoria Blakemore

vblakemore.author@gmail.com

Copyright info/picture credits

Cover, Panupon Eurawong/Shutterstock; Page 3, Meister Photos/Shutterstock; Page 5, Gerty Vrey/AdobeStock; Page 7, anankkml /AdobeStock; Page 9, 169169/Adobestock; Pages 10-11, Dmitry Pichugin/AdobeStock; Page 13, michael luckett /AdobeStock; Page 15, Pb/AdobeStock; Page 17, hugy/AdobeStock; Page 19, Angiolo/AdobeStock; Page 21, Megan Paine/AdobeStock; Page 23; Sky/AdobeStock; Page 25, 12019/Pixabay; Page 27, NMint/AdobeStock; Page 29, Danita Delimont/AdobeStock; Page 31, Dmitry/AdobeStock; Page 33, Panupon Eurawong/Shutterstock

Table of Contents

What Are Crocodiles?

Crocodiles are large reptiles. They are from the same family as alligators and caimans.

There are 14 different kinds of true crocodiles. They differ in their size and where they live. The Nile crocodile and the saltwater crocodile are the most common crocodiles.

Crocodiles are known for being **aggressive**. The crocodiles of Australia and Africa are the most **aggressive** of the crocodile species.

Size

The largest kind of crocodile is the saltwater crocodile. It is usually between 16 and 20 feet long. It can weigh around 2,000 pounds.

The smallest kind of crocodile is the dwarf caiman. It is usually between 4 and 5 feet long. It weighs less than 16 pounds.

Male crocodiles are larger than female crocodiles. They also usually have thicker tails.

Crocodiles have hard, scaly skin. It has bony plates inside that protect the crocodile like an armor.

They have webbed feet. The webbing between the toes helps to **propel** them through the water. Their strong tail also **propels** them as they swim.

Crocodiles have eyes on the top of their head. This lets them see what is going on above the water while the rest of their body is hidden.

Habitat

Crocodiles live in saltwater and **brackish** environments like ponds, lakes, creeks, wetlands, and canals.

They have a special gland that allows them to get rid of extra salt, which is why they can live in salty water.

Range

Crocodiles are found in Asia, Africa, Australia, and the Americas.

The country with the most crocodiles is Australia. There are over 100,000 crocodiles there.

Diet

Crocodiles are **carnivores**.

They only eat meat.

Their diet is made up of fish, birds, small mammals, and frogs. Larger crocodiles may also eat larger mammals such as zebras and wildebeests.

Crocodiles stay hidden in the water, then lunge out to catch their prey when it is close enough.

Crocodiles can't chew food like other animals. They use their sharp teeth to crush their prey, which they then swallow whole.

Since they can't break off pieces of food, crocodiles swallow small stones that help to break down the food in their stomach.

When crocodiles lose a tooth,

another tooth grows in to

replace it.

Communication

Crocodiles use sound, scent, and movement to communicate.

Male crocodiles can be very **territorial**. They do not like other males getting close. They may slap the water with their tail or lunge at other males to scare them off.

Crocodiles make sounds like growls, hisses, and roars. Many of these sounds are used to warn others away.

Movement

Crocodiles can run quite fast for short distances. They have been recorded running at speeds of up to twenty miles per hour.

They are good swimmers and can swim about eighteen miles per hour. They use their strong tail to **propel** them through the water.

Crocodiles walk along the ground underwater. They can stay underwater for about an hour before coming up for air.

Young Crocodiles

Crocodiles build a mound of dirt near the water's edge. Then, they lay up to fifty eggs. The eggs hatch after a few months.

Mother crocodiles take care of young crocodiles until they are old enough to hunt. They keep them safe from other crocodiles.

Crocodiles carry their babies on their backs or in their mouth when the babies are little.

Crocodile Life

Crocodiles are mostly **nocturnal**.

They are most active at night.

They spend their days resting in

the sun or floating in the water.

Crocodiles often live in groups.

These groups are called "basks"

when they are on land. They

are called "floats" in the water.

Groups of crocodiles are often seen on land, warming themselves up in the sun.

Crocodile or Alligator?

Alligators live in fresh water.

They cannot **regulate** the

amount of salt in their bodies

like crocodiles can.

Crocodiles have a snout that

is more narrow and pointed.

Alligator snouts are wider and

more rounded.

Unlike crocodiles, alligators do

not have many visible teeth.

Their teeth are mostly hidden

until they open their mouth.

Population

Of the 14 species of true crocodiles, 5 are **endangered** or **critically endangered**. This includes the Cuban crocodile and the Siamese crocodile.

The other 9 species are either not **endangered**, or their populations have not been **assessed**.

Crocodiles have a long
lifespan. They can live up to
seventy years in the wild.

Crocodiles in Danger

One of the main threats that crocodiles are facing is habitat destruction. Many habitats are being cleared for buildings, roads, and farming.

Rising water temperatures can affect crocodile habitats. When people drain wetlands, crocodiles can lose their habitat.

Crocodiles are hunted for their hides. Their hides are used to make things like shoes, purses, and belts.

Helping Crocodiles

Many research groups are working to study crocodiles. They track their movements to find out where they go. They also study their behavior.

Understanding what crocodiles do and where they are can help researchers come up with ways to help them.

In some places, wildlife **preserves** provide animals like crocodiles with safe places to live. They are safe from habitat loss there.

Education is also a big part of helping crocodiles. Learning how to live alongside crocodiles can keep both people and crocodiles safe.

Glossary

Aggressive: mean, ready to fight or attack

Assessed: to determine the amount of

Brackish: a bit salty

Carnivore: an animal that eats only meat

Critically endangered: when an animal is almost extinct

Declining: getting smaller

Endangered: at risk of becoming extinct

Extinct: when there are no more of an animal left in the wild

Nocturnal: animals that are active and

night

Predator: an animal that hunts other

animals for food

Preserves: areas of land set up to

protect plants and animals

Propel: to push forward

Regulate: to control, to adjust

Territorial: when an animal is

protective of its territory

Victoria Blakemore is a first grade

teacher in Southwest Florida with a

passion for reading.

You can visit her at

www.enchantedinelementary.com

Also in This Series

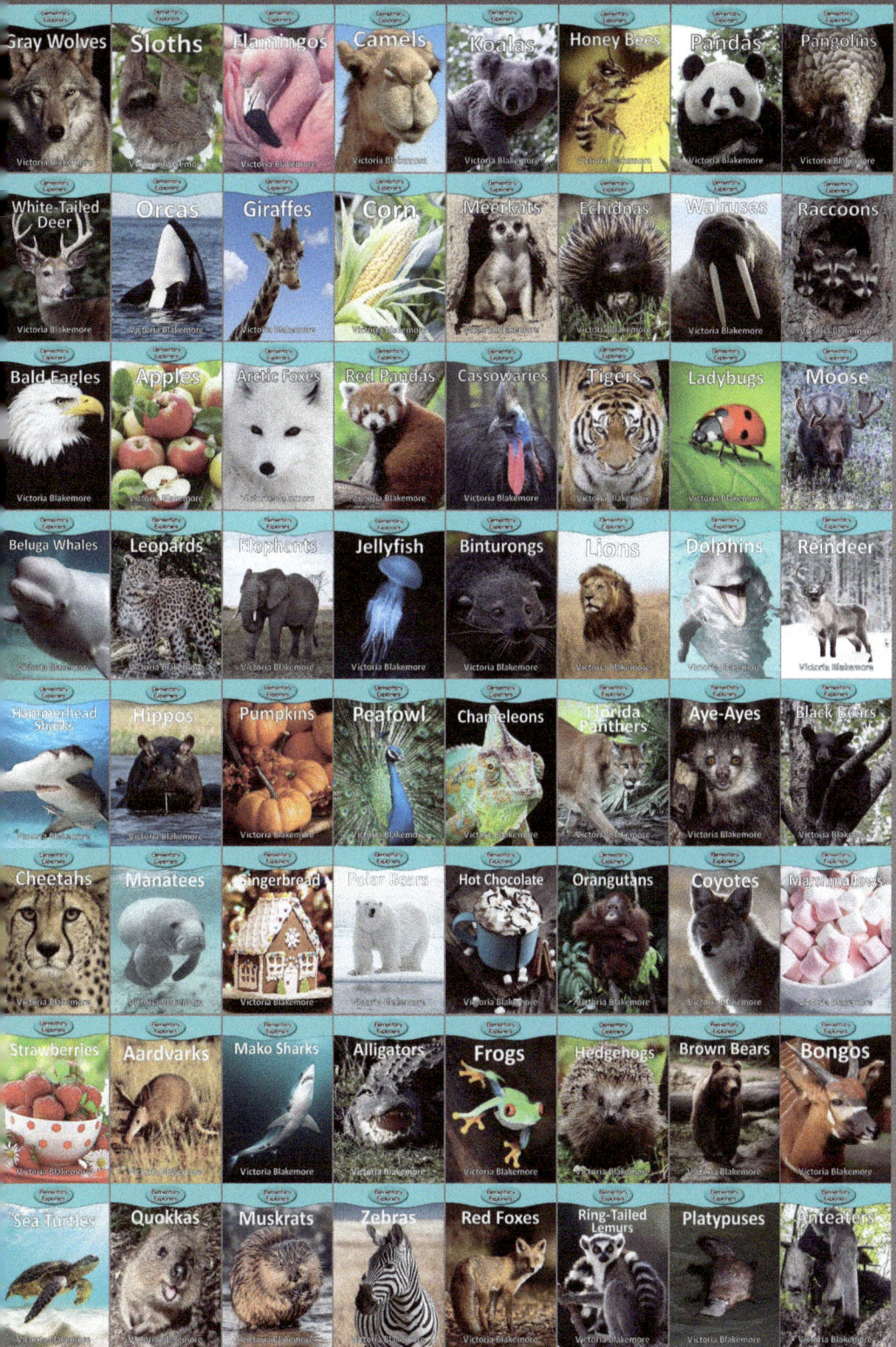

Gray Wolves	Sloths	Flamingos	Camels	Koalas	Honey Bees	Pandas	Pangolins
White-Tailed Deer	Orcas	Giraffes	Corn	Meerkats	Echidnas	Walruses	Raccoons
Bald Eagles	Apples	Arctic Foxes	Red Pandas	Cassowaries	Tigers	Ladybugs	Moose
Beluga Whales	Leopards	Elephants	Jellyfish	Binturongs	Lions	Dolphins	Reindeer
Hammerhead Sharks	Hippos	Pumpkins	Peafowl	Chameleons	Florida Panthers	Aye-Ayes	Black Bears
Cheetahs	Manatees	Gingerbread	Polar Bears	Hot Chocolate	Orangutans	Coyotes	Marshmallows
Strawberries	Aardvarks	Mako Sharks	Alligators	Frogs	Hedgehogs	Brown Bears	Bongos
Sea Turtles	Quokkas	Muskrats	Zebras	Red Foxes	Ring-Tailed Lemurs	Platypuses	Anteaters

Also in This Series

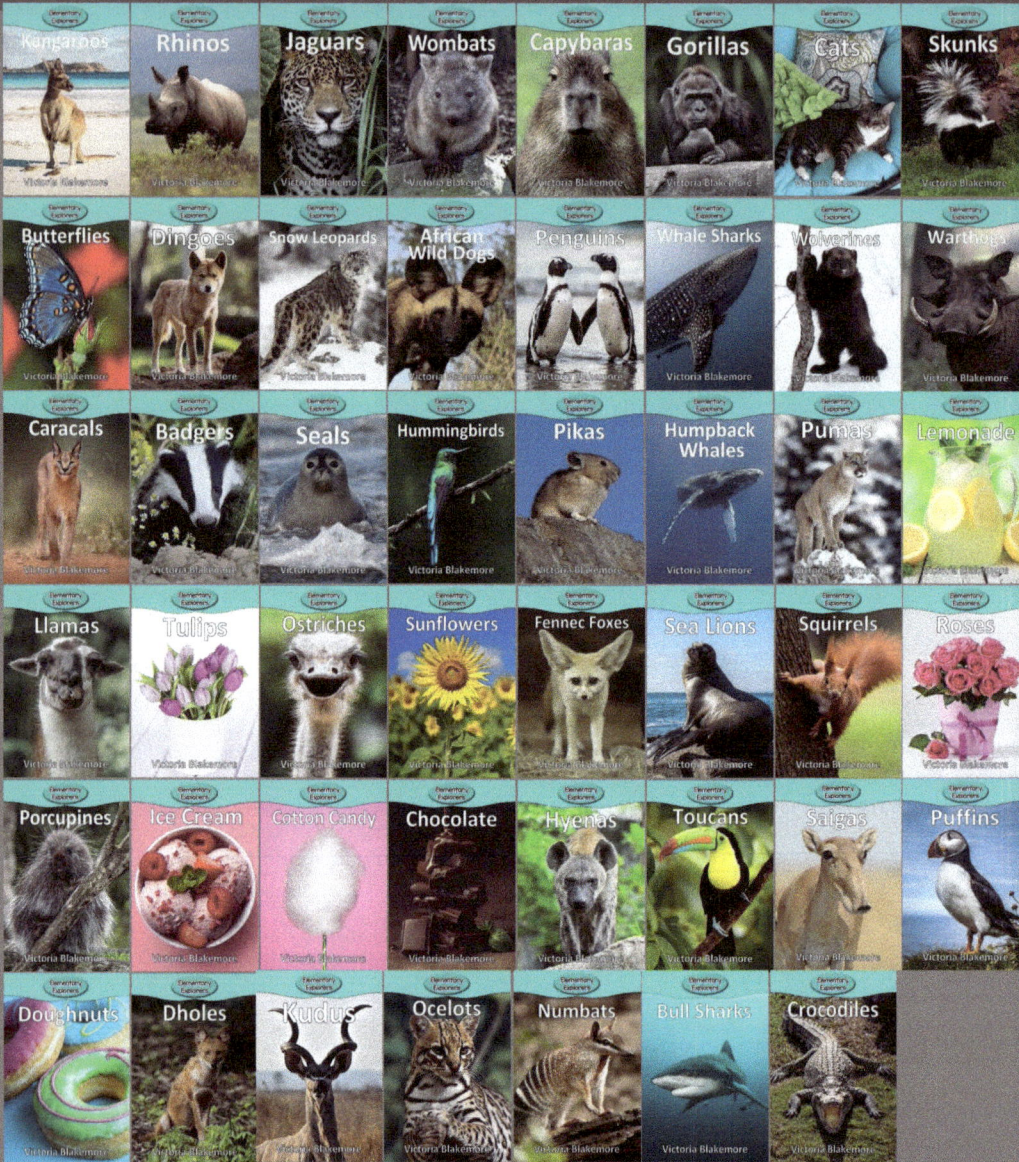

Kangaroos · Rhinos · Jaguars · Wombats · Capybaras · Gorillas · Cats · Skunks

Butterflies · Dingoes · Snow Leopards · African Wild Dogs · Penguins · Whale Sharks · Wolverines · Warthogs

Caracals · Badgers · Seals · Hummingbirds · Pikas · Humpback Whales · Pumas · Lemonade

Llamas · Tulips · Ostriches · Sunflowers · Fennec Foxes · Sea Lions · Squirrels · Roses

Porcupines · Ice Cream · Cotton Candy · Chocolate · Hyenas · Toucans · Saigas · Puffins

Doughnuts · Dholes · Kudus · Ocelots · Numbats · Bull Sharks · Crocodiles

www.ingramcontent.com/pod-product-compliance
Lightning Source LLC
Chambersburg PA
CBHW052124030426
42335CB00025B/3108